Saving Your SECOND MARRIAGE

Before It Starts

Nine Questions

to Ask Before

(and After) You Remarry

Drs. Les and Leslie Parrott

ZONDERVAN™

GRAND RAPIDS, MICHIGAN 49530

We want to hear from you. Please send your comments about this
book to us in care of the address below. Thank you.

GRAND RAPIDS, MICHIGAN 49530

w w w . z o n d e r v a n . c o m

ZONDERVAN™

Saving Your Second Marriage Before It Starts Workbook for Men
Copyright © 2001 by Les and Leslie Parrott

Requests for information should be addressed to:

Zondervan, *Grand Rapids, Michigan 49530*

ISBN 0-310-24054-9

Printed in the United States of America

01 02 03 04 05 06 /❖ EP/ 10 9 8 7 6 5 4 3 2 1

Contents

How to Use This Workbook

We have seen many couples who marry and then wait to see what will happen. This workbook is a tool to help you make the *right* things happen. Its brief exercises and activities, to be completed as you read through *Saving Your Second Marriage Before It Starts*, come from our work in counseling couples and are proven strategies for enriching and developing your relationship. Too often, reading a book can lead to great ideas, but little action. This workbook will help you put feet on the ideas and put them into action. And we believe you will enjoy it! As Shakespeare said, "Joy's soul lies in the doing."

This workbook is to be used in conjunction with your wife's—there is one designed for men and one for women—and it is important that each of you have your own copy. For the best results, each of you should work on the exercises separately, then meet together to discuss your answers.

While there is no one right way to use this workbook, we suggest that you complete the exercises as you encounter them in the book, or soon after you have finished reading the chapter that covers the exercise. In other words, try to complete the exercises for that chapter before moving on to the next one. The point is to integrate the exercises into the process of reading the book. Some of the exercises are designed to be used again and again, helping you continue to improve your communication, for example, or deepen your sense of intimacy. Others are more of a one-shot exercise and are exploratory in nature.

As you work through the pages of this book, make it your own. Don't get too hung up on following the rules. If a particular exercise leads you down a more intriguing path, take it. Some of these exercises may simply serve as springboards to discussions that fit your style more appropriately. However, if an exercise seems a bit challenging, don't give up on it. As the saying goes, anything worth having is worth working for. In any case, the goal of this workbook is not simply to fortify your reading of *Saving Your Second Marriage Before It Starts*—the goal is to apply it, to make it real.

Exercise One:
The Remarriage Motivation Test

On a scale of 1 to 10, rate how much of a factor each of the following motivators are for you to get married. Take time to consider each item, and be as honest as possible.

1. Love at first sight is a factor in why I'm ready to get married again.

Not at All True   *Extremely True of Me*
1   2   3   4   5   6   7   8   9   10

2. Rebounding from the pain of a previous marriage is a factor in my motivation for this second marriage.

Not at All True   *Extremely True of Me*
1   2   3   4   5   6   7   8   9   10

3. Rebellion against my ex-wife is a factor in my motivation.

Not at All True   *Extremely True of Me*
1   2   3   4   5   6   7   8   9   10

4. Loneliness contributes to my reasons for getting married again.

Not at All True   *Extremely True of Me*
1   2   3   4   5   6   7   8   9   10

5. A sense of obligation is a factor in motivating me to marry.

Not at All True   *Extremely True of Me*
1   2   3   4   5   6   7   8   9   10

6. Financial advancement is a part of my decision to get remarried.

Not at All True   *Extremely True of Me*
1   2   3   4   5   6   7   8   9   10

7. Sexual attraction is a factor driving me to get married at this time.

Not at All True   *Extremely True of Me*
1   2   3   4   5   6   7   8   9   10

8. Escape from an unhappy first marriage is causing me to want to get married again.

Not at All True   *Extremely True of Me*

1   2   3   4   5   6   7   8   9   10

9. Pressure from others has something to do with why I am getting married again.

Not at All True   *Extremely True of Me*

1   2   3   4   5   6   7   8   9   10

Scoring: Add up your score from each of the nine items. There are ninety possible points on this test. Add ten to your score. If your score is fifteen or less, you can rest easy in the fact that you are probably not getting remarried for some of the most common negative reasons. If your score is greater than fifteen, you will certainly want to do some soul-searching on your own and with your partner about the items that you ranked highest. We also strongly suggest talking about these motivators with an objective counselor.

EXERCISE TWO:
The Remarriage Readiness Questionnaire

The following questions will help you assess your readiness for remarriage. Be ruthlessly honest with yourself while answering these questions.

1. Do you know who you are and do you like who you are?
2. Would you say you generally have a healthy sense of self-esteem and confidence?
3. Do you feel comfortable talking about your differences in times of conflict (rather than ignoring them)?
4. Are you twenty years of age or older?
5. Are you twenty-four years of age or older?
6. Would people you respect say you are personally mature?
7. Would you say you have resolved most of the ugly issues with your former wife?
8. Do you feel comfortable thinking for yourself and making your own decisions?
9. Are you able to make decisions without feeling compelled to please others?
10. Are you genuinely prepared to make your marriage relationship of utmost priority?
11. Have you resolved painful or other troubling issues with your past that are bound to impact your new marriage?
12. Have you identified specific quirks or qualities you may be bringing into your marriage as a result of your previous relationship?
13. Have you dated your partner for a year or more?
14. Have you dated your partner for two years or more?

15. Are you willing to take your time in determining whether your relationship is really ready for marriage?
16. Would you characterize your relationship as stable and steadfast?
17. Do you both practice compromise and negotiation effectively in your relationship?
18. Can you both resolve conflict between you without losing control?
19. Are you 100 percent committed, beyond a shadow of a doubt, to making this relationship work?
20. Does your partner have any important goals or values with which you do not agree?
21. Do you and your partner share many similarities (e.g., sense of humor, habits, goals)?
22. Are your differences tiny compared to your similarities?
23. Do you and your partner have similar family backgrounds?
24. Do you and your partner refrain from criticizing, correcting, or trying to "fix" each other?
25. Do you like this person as she is at this moment (as compared to expecting her to change)?

Scoring: Add up the number of yes responses from these items and multiply by four. That will give you a possible score of 100. If you answered honestly and your score is 90 or higher, your answers indicate you are probably ready for remarriage. A score of 80 to 89 indicates that you are on your way but would probably be wise to give it more time and careful counsel. A score of 79 or lower indicates that you still have a great deal of work to do before you are ready for remarriage. You are likely to benefit from the help of a good counselor and more time. Whether your score is high or low, this brief self-report assessment should serve simply as a guideline, not as the final answer.

Exercise Three:

Your Personal Ten Commandments

This exercise is designed to help you uncover some of your unspoken rules. It will take about fifteen to twenty minutes.

Try to articulate some of the unspoken rules you grew up with. Take your time to think it over. These unspoken rules are generally so ingrained that we are rarely aware of them.

Once both of you have articulated your "personal ten commandments," share them with each other. Are there rules you would like to change? Take a moment to discuss how unspoken rules might affect your marriage.

1. _____

_____

2. _____

_____

3. _____

_____

4. _____

_____

5. _____

_____

6. _____

_____

7. _____

_____

8. _____

_____

9. _____

_____

10. _____

_____

Anytime you have a fight or disagreement, ask yourself: "Is this fight a result of one of us breaking an unspoken rule?" If so, add that rule to your list, and discuss with your wife how you will handle that situation in the future.

EXERCISE FOUR:
Making Your Roles Conscious

Listed below are a number of chores or life tasks that will need to be handled by you or your wife. To make your unconscious understanding of roles conscious, first indicate how your parents handled these tasks. Then write down how you would like to divide up the tasks, according to your understanding of your own and your wife's interests, time, and abilities. Finally, compare your list with your wife's list and discuss the results. Put your final decision of who will do what in the last column, and be prepared to renegotiate when your circumstances change. This exercise will take about thirty minutes.

	Your Mother	Your Father	Both Parents	You	Your Spouse	Both of You	Final Decision
Providing income	❏	❏	❏	❏	❏	❏	_____
Staying home with children	❏	❏	❏	❏	❏	❏	_____
Handling finances	❏	❏	❏	❏	❏	❏	_____
Yard work	❏	❏	❏	❏	❏	❏	_____
Automobile care	❏	❏	❏	❏	❏	❏	_____
Laundry	❏	❏	❏	❏	❏	❏	_____
Dishes	❏	❏	❏	❏	❏	❏	_____
Cleaning	❏	❏	❏	❏	❏	❏	_____
Cooking and baking	❏	❏	❏	❏	❏	❏	_____
Grocery shopping	❏	❏	❏	❏	❏	❏	_____
Caring for pet	❏	❏	❏	❏	❏	❏	_____
Scheduling social events	❏	❏	❏	❏	❏	❏	_____
Maintaining ties with friends and relatives	❏	❏	❏	❏	❏	❏	_____
Planning vacations	❏	❏	❏	❏	❏	❏	_____
Initiating sex	❏	❏	❏	❏	❏	❏	_____
Decorating the house	❏	❏	❏	❏	❏	❏	_____

	Your Mother	Your Father	Both Parents	You	Your Spouse	Both of You	Final Decision
Making major decisions	❏	❏	❏	❏	❏	❏	_____
Initiating discussion about the relationship	❏	❏	❏	❏	❏	❏	_____
Keeping the house neat and orderly	❏	❏	❏	❏	❏	❏	_____
Disciplining the children	❏	❏	❏	❏	❏	❏	_____
Shopping for other needs	❏	❏	❏	❏	❏	❏	_____
Other	❏	❏	❏	❏	❏	❏	_____
Other	❏	❏	❏	❏	❏	❏	_____

Note: We believe that some of these tasks (such as disciplining children or initiating sex) must be shared in order for the couple to have a strong relationship, but in reality many of the tasks may fall disproportionately to the husband or the wife because of unspoken assumptions or circumstances. Use this list periodically to discuss how you are doing and readjust your roles or assignments if you need to.

Exercise Five:
From Idealizing to Realizing Your Partner

This exercise is designed to help you relinquish unrealistic ideals you might hold of your wife and to discover her true character. It will take about twenty-five to thirty minutes.

Begin by ranking on a one-to-seven scale how much the following traits describe you and your wife. Complete the first two columns ("Your Ranking of You" and then "Your Ranking of Your Wife"). Don't worry about the other two columns just yet.

Your Ranking of You		Your Ranking of Your Wife		Your Wife's Actual Rank		The Difference
____	compassionate	____	-	____	=	____
____	patient	____	-	____	=	____
____	secure	____	-	____	=	____
____	nurturing	____	-	____	=	____
____	insightful	____	-	____	=	____
____	confident	____	-	____	=	____
____	relaxed	____	-	____	=	____
____	tender	____	-	____	=	____
____	even tempered	____	-	____	=	____
____	honest	____	-	____	=	____
____	healthy	____	-	____	=	____
____	spiritual	____	-	____	=	____
____	consistent	____	-	____	=	____

Once you have ranked the first two columns, share your rankings with each other and write them on your own page. Then subtract your wife's actual ranking of herself from your ranking of her. Note any significant differences and discuss them.

One of the central tasks of the early marriage years is to move from "idealizing" your wife to "realizing" your wife. How accurate is your image of who your wife is compared to who she really is? The more accurately you can present yourselves to each other, the easier your first years of marriage will be.

EXERCISE SIX:
Exploring Unfinished Business

Marriage is not a quick fix for avoiding your own personal problems. In fact, marriage may even intensify those problems. This exercise is designed to help you honestly face the psychological and spiritual work you need to do as a person so that you do not look to your wife to fulfill needs that she cannot fulfill. It will take about twenty to thirty minutes.

Everyone has yearnings that were seldom if ever fulfilled in their relationship with their parents. Take a moment to reflect, and then write down some of the needs and desires you felt that were never really fulfilled by your parents or by your first wife.

_____

_____

_____

_____

_____

_____

_____

_____

_____

_____

_____

_____

_____

_____

_____

_____

_____

When we marry, we long to recreate the love and closeness and nurturance that we experienced or wished we had experienced in our relationship with our parents. But marriage is not always the place for those yearnings to be fulfilled. No human can meet another person's every need; deep relational longings are ultimately met only in a relationship with God.

If you are willing, share your writing with your wife and discuss the baggage you are both bringing into your marriage.

Exercise Seven:
Assessing Your Self-Image

This exercise is designed to help you measure your self-image and construct an interdependent relationship with your wife. It will take about twenty to thirty minutes.

"You cannot love another person unless you love yourself." Most of us have heard that statement so often we tend to dismiss it as just another catchphrase in the lexicon of pop psychology. But a solid sense of self-esteem is a vital element in building the capacity to love.

The following self-test can give you a quick evaluation of your self-esteem. Answer each with "yes," "usually," "seldom," or "no."

1. Do you believe strongly in certain values and principles, so that you are willing to defend them?

   ❏ Yes ❏ Usually ❏ Seldom ❏ No

2. Do you act on your own best judgment, without regretting your actions if others disapprove?

   ❏ Yes ❏ Usually ❏ Seldom ❏ No

3. Do you avoid worrying about what is coming tomorrow or fussing over yesterday's or today's mistakes?

   ❏ Yes ❏ Usually ❏ Seldom ❏ No

4. Do you have confidence in your general ability to deal with problems, even in the face of failures and setbacks?

   ❏ Yes ❏ Usually ❏ Seldom ❏ No

5. Do you feel generally equal—neither inferior nor superior—to others?

   ❏ Yes ❏ Usually ❏ Seldom ❏ No

6. Do you take it more or less for granted that other people are interested in you and value you?

   ❏ Yes ❏ Usually ❏ Seldom ❏ No

7. Do you accept praise without pretense or false modesty, and accept compliments without feeling guilty?

   ❒ Yes   ❒ Usually   ❒ Seldom   ❒ No

8. Do you resist the efforts of others to dominate you, especially your peers?

   ❒ Yes   ❒ Usually   ❒ Seldom   ❒ No

9. Do you accept the idea—and admit to others—that you are capable of feeling a wide range of impulses and desires, ranging from anger to love, sadness to happiness, resentment to acceptance? (It does not follow, however, that you will act on all these feelings and desires.)

   ❒ Yes   ❒ Usually   ❒ Seldom   ❒ No

10. Do you genuinely enjoy yourself in a wide range of activities, including work, play, creative self-expression, companionship, and just plain loafing?

    ❒ Yes   ❒ Usually   ❒ Seldom   ❒ No

11. Do you sense and consider the needs of others?

    ❒ Yes   ❒ Usually   ❒ Seldom   ❒ No

If your answer to most of the questions are "yes" or "usually," you probably have high self-esteem. If most of your answers were "no" or "seldom," you may likely suffer from a low self-image and thus will need to strengthen it to build the best marriage. Research indicates that self-esteem has a lot to do with the way you will respond to your wife. People with a healthy self-image are more apt to express their opinions, are less sensitive to criticism, and are generally less preoccupied with themselves.

Exercise Eight:
Defining Love

This exercise will help you define love in your own terms and compare your definition with your wife's. It will take fifteen to twenty minutes.

Researcher Beverly Fehr asked more than 170 people to rate the central features of love. The twelve most important attributes they identified are listed below. Take a moment to prioritize this list for yourself.

____ acceptance

____ caring

____ commitment

____ concern for the other's well-being

____ friendship

____ honesty

____ interest in the other

____ loyalty

____ respect

____ supportiveness

____ trust

____ wanting to be with the other

Next, circle your top three attributes of love and write a definition of love that incorporates them.

Love is ...

_____

_____

_____

_____

_____

_____

_____

_____

_____

_____

Now compare your priorities and your definition with your wife's to see what differences, if any, you might have when it comes to defining love. How has your definition of love changed since your first marriage?

Exercise Nine:
Your Changing Love Style

This exercise will help you understand how love is not stagnant and how the love you have for each other will change during different life passages. It will take twenty-five to thirty minutes.

Using the triangular model of love described in chapter 2 (passion, intimacy, and commitment), draw how your love style with your wife has changed over time. You may want to divide your relationship into three phases and then draw the love triangle that best suits each phase.

As we grow and develop, each stage of the life cycle is marked by the emergence of a new form of love. This means that during certain phases of life, some sides of the triangle will get more attention than others. Using the triangular model of love, draw how your love might look in future passages of marriage, especially if you are blending children into your second marriage.

Discuss with your wife how you feel about the inevitability of love taking on different forms in your future.

EXERCISE TEN:
Cultivating Intimacy

This exercise will help you open your heart and increase your level of intimacy. It will take about sixty minutes.

Begin by writing about your shared experiences. What is it about your backgrounds that draws you together? What things set the two of you apart from others? What experiences have you had together that bring back fond memories?

_____

_____

_____

_____

_____

_____

_____

Next, focus on things that the two of you share. Begin by jotting down one or two things in each of the following categories, then discuss them with your wife. The more detailed you can be, the better.

• Interests we have in common include:

_____

_____

_____

- Plans we share for our future include:

_____

_____

_____

- Fears and anxieties we both have include:

_____

_____

_____

- Hopes and dreams we share include:

_____

_____

_____

- Spiritual beliefs we both have include:

_____

_____

_____

Conclude this exercise by talking in specific terms about what the two of you can do to cultivate more emotional intimacy in your relationship.

EXERCISE ELEVEN:
Listening to Your Self-Talk

This exercise will help you and your wife examine how much your attitude shapes the moods of your marriage. It will take about ten to fifteen minutes.

List three circumstances that typically get you into a rotten mood. For example: being stuck in traffic, waiting for someone to arrive who is late, having your credit card rejected, and so on.

1. _____

2. _____

3. _____

There is a maxim in psychology that says "you feel what you think." In other words, your feelings are the result of what is going on in your mind. For each of the bad circumstances you listed above, write down what you are saying to yourself that makes you feel so rotten. For example: "I could be playing tennis instead of being stuck on this freeway."

1. _____

2. _____

3. _____

Now, exercise your power to choose your own attitude by changing your self-talk. Write three alternative statements that would not lead to feeling so rotten. For example: "At least I can use this time to just relax and mentally rehearse my tennis serve."

1. _____

2. _____

3. _____

Negative self-talk can also affect our response to more serious situations. To see how negative self-talk may have affected you, list two situations in your life that were difficult or painful to deal with. For example: losing a job, going through a divorce, or going through a serious illness.

1. _____

2. _____

For each of the crises you listed above, write down things you said to yourself that added to your pain. For example: "I was fired from my job because I'm a natural-born loser."

1. _____

_____

2. _____

_____

Again, exercise your power to choose your own attitude by changing your self-talk. Write two alternative statements that did help or could have helped you adapt to the situation and grow through it. For example: "I will learn from my mistakes and, with God's help, make sure they don't happen again."

1. _____

_____

2. _____

_____

Talk about this exercise with your wife. Discuss how changing your self-talk can improve your chances for marital happiness. How can the two of you team up to fight negative self-talk?

EXERCISE TWELVE:
Avoiding the Blame Game

This exercise will help you and your wife take responsibility for your own attitudes. It will take about ten to fifteen minutes.

Below are several scenarios where blame typically enters the picture. For each scenario, decide on your own who is to blame.

First Scene

It's Valentine's Day. Mary has prepared a special meal for Dan—all his favorite foods. She also made him a special Valentine. Dan, however, didn't get Mary anything. After dinner, Dan thanks Mary for the food and slumps into a chair in front of the television. Mary, feeling hurt, leaves the dirty dishes in the sink and goes into the bedroom to cry. Dan realizes what just happened, follows her into the bedroom, and the two accuse each other of being insensitive. Who is at fault?

Dan is to blame   Mary is to blame

|—+—+—+—+—+—+—+—+—+—|

Second Scene

Aaron and Kim are having dinner with another couple. During the casual conversation, Kim jokingly makes fun of Aaron's shirt. He laughs at first, but soon he becomes withdrawn, and the conversation becomes noticeably strained. When they get home, both of them accuse the other of ruining the evening. Who is at fault?

Aaron is to blame   Kim is to blame

|—+—+—+—+—+—+—+—+—+—|

Third Scene

On a whim, Carl buys a new CD player on sale. He and Michelle had talked about getting one, but they'd decided to wait another year. Carl, however, felt the bargain was too good to pass up and also thought it would be a nice surprise for Michelle. It wasn't. All Michelle could think about was how they were saving money for plane tickets to see her family at Christmas. Carl and Michelle blamed each other for being too controlling with their money. Who is at fault?

Carl is to blame   Michelle is to blame

You may now compare your answers with each other, but there are no "correct" responses. It doesn't matter who is to blame. It doesn't matter who is at fault. What matters in building a happy marriage is defining what the problem is and seeing how each of you can be a part of the solution. Take time to read through the scenarios again, placing yourselves in the couple's shoes. What could each of you do to avoid playing the blame game in these instances?

_____

_____

_____

_____

_____

_____

_____

_____

_____

EXERCISE THIRTEEN:
Adjusting to Things Beyond Your Control

This exercise will help you and your wife more effectively adjust to the jolts of life. It will take about ten to fifteen minutes.

The book talked about how different the Christmas story would be if Mary and Joseph had not had the capacity to adjust to circumstances beyond their control. What situations or circumstances in your wedding and marriage have already thrown you for a loop? Jot down two or three particular challenges you did not anticipate:

_____

_____

_____

_____

_____

How did you respond to these unexpected situations? List some things you did to keep your chin up and some things you did that didn't work as well.

Positive Ways I Coped	*Negative Ways I Coped*
_____	_____
_____	_____
_____	_____
_____	_____
_____	_____

Now compare your coping strategies with your wife's. In what ways can the two of you improve your capacities to adjust? How can you be better equipped to maintain a positive outlook when similar unexpected circumstances arise in the future?

Conclude this exercise by discussing what will happen in your marriage if you do not practice your ability to adjust to things beyond your control.

EXERCISE FOURTEEN:
How Well Do You Communicate?

This self-test is designed to help you assess how well you communicate with your wife. It will take about ten minutes. Answer the questions as honestly as you can. The more honest you are, the more meaningful the exercise will be.

1. When your wife is in a bad mood, you are likely to:
   A. Ask whether she's getting her period.
   B. Leave her alone until she's feeling better.
   C. Ask her what's wrong.

2. She says you don't tell her often enough that you love her. You reply:
   A. "I tell you I love you all the time."
   B. "You know I love you. Why do I have to say it?"
   C. "I love you very much. Sometimes I just forget to say so."

3. You are watching television, and she says she'd like to talk to you. You say:
   A. "How about ten o'clock?"
   B. "Anytime you want."
   C. "Sorry, I'm in the middle of something right now."

4. How often do you win arguments with your wife?
   A. Almost always.
   B. Almost never.
   C. I try not to think in terms of winning or losing.

5. Your wife wants to talk about some difficulties she is having at work. Would you most likely:
   A. Point out that you have work problems of your own?
   B. Offer helpful advice?
   C. Listen and try to be supportive?

6. For the second time this week you find that she didn't run an errand as she had promised. Annoyed, you:
   A. Tell her how much it irritates you and do it yourself.
   B. Pout a bit and ask her to do it tomorrow.
   C. "Forget" to do something for her next time she asks.

7. You're in a romantic mood, but when you reach for her she just yawns. You:
   A. Feel rejected and say, "Woo, it's cold in here."
   B. Ask her why she isn't responding.
   C. Let her know your desires but adjust if she is not in sync.

Scoring: For questions one, two, four, five, and seven, give yourself one point for each "A" answer, two for each "B," and three for each "C." Then on questions three and six give yourself three points for each "A," two for each "B," and one for each "C."

7 to 11 points: Hiding your feelings is one of the fastest ways you can ruin a relationship. You need to learn how to listen to your wife and how to talk with her. Chapter 6 will show you how.

12 to 17 points: You're doing well, but you need to remember that your wife needs your support and encouragement much more than she needs your advice. You can really benefit from practicing some of the skills discussed in chapter 6.

18 to 21 points: You're doing quite well in the area of communication, but there's always room for improvement. Chapter 6 will help you fine-tune some skills you are already good at.

EXERCISE FIFTEEN:
The Daily Temperature Reading

This exercise will help you and your wife maintain an easy flow of communication about the big and little things going on in your lives. It will take about thirty minutes.

At first this exercise may seem artificial and even hokey. But in time you'll evolve your own style and find that it is invaluable for staying close. Do it daily, perhaps during a meal. Here are the basics. Sit close, holding each other's hands (touch creates an atmosphere of acceptance), then follow these five steps:

1. *Appreciation*. Take turns expressing appreciation for something your spouse has done. Thank each other.

2. *New Information*. In the absence of information, assumptions (often false ones) rush in. Tell your spouse something new ("We finally got a new account executive at work."). Let your spouse in on your life. And then listen to the news your spouse shares.

3. *Puzzles*. Take turns asking each other something you don't understand but your spouse can explain: "Why were you so down last night?" Or voice a concern about yourself: "I don't know why I got so angry while I was balancing the checkbook yesterday."

4. *Complaint with Request*. Without being judgmental, cite a specific behavior that bothers you and state the behavior you are asking for instead. "When you clean the top of the stove, please dry it with a paper towel. If you don't, it leaves streaks."

5. *Hopes*. Share your hopes, from the mundane ("I hope we have sunshine this weekend.") to the grandiose ("I'd really love to spend a month in Europe with you.").

These simple steps have worked for many couples who want to keep the channels of communication open.

Exercise Sixteen:
I Can Hear Clearly Now

Your wife will often hide important feelings behind her words. Reflecting her feelings is one of the most helpful and diffcult listening techniques to implement. Following are some statements that a wife might make. Read each separately, listening for feelings. Make note of the feeling you hear and write out a response which reflects that feeling for each of the statements.

1. "I don't want your advice!"

    _____

2. "Karen doesn't seem to call me like she used to."

    _____

3. "I am so tired of never knowing when you are going to get home."

    _____

4. "I'd like to ask for a raise, but what if I don't get it?"

    _____

5. "Just once I'd like not to have to pick your coat off this chair."

    _____

Now compare your list of reflective statements to those listed below to see how accurately you recognized feelings. Give yourself a 2 on those items where your choice closely matches, a 1 on items where your choice only partially matches, and a 0 if you missed altogether.

Possible Reponses to the Exercise in Active Listening:

1. "Sounds like you'd just like to be understood."
2. "You must feel kind of hurt."
3. "You sound so frustrated; let's work this thing out."
4. "Sounds like you are feeling anxious and a little afraid."
5. "That's got to be aggravating. I'll make it a point not to do that so much."

How you rate on recognizing feelings:

8–10 Above average recognition of feelings

5–7 Average recognition of feelings

0–4 Below average recognition of feelings

EXERCISE SEVENTEEN:
Couple's Inventory

This exercise will help you take stock of the roles you both play, consciously and unconsciously, in your relationship. It will take about twenty to thirty minutes.

Complete the following sentences as honestly as you can.

1. I am important to our marriage because

   _____

2. What I contribute to my wife's success is

   _____

3. I feel central to our relationship when

   _____

4. I feel peripheral to our relationship when

   _____

5. The ways I have fun with you are

   _____

6. The way I get space for myself in our relationship is

   _____

7. The ways I am intimate with you are

   _____

8. The role I play as your husband is

   _____

9. I feel most masculine in our relationship when

   _____

10. I deal with stress by

   _____

11. The division of labor in household tasks is decided by

_____

12. Our finances are controlled by

_____

13. How we spend our spare time is determined by

_____

14. Our social life is planned by

_____

15. I need you to

_____

Compare your statements with each other and discuss how your gender influences the way you responded.

EXERCISE EIGHTEEN:
Your Top Ten Needs

This exercise will help you identify some of your deepest needs in a marriage relationship and communicate those needs to your wife. It will take about twenty to thirty minutes.

Listed below are some of the most common needs that people identify as being important in marriage. Rate how important each of these items is for you. If you wish to add other items not included in our list, please do so. As always, do this on your own before discussing it with your wife.

	Not that important						*Very Important*
Admiration	1	2	3	4	5	6	7
Affection	1	2	3	4	5	6	7
Commitment	1	2	3	4	5	6	7
Companionship	1	2	3	4	5	6	7
Conversation	1	2	3	4	5	6	7
Financial support	1	2	3	4	5	6	7
Honesty	1	2	3	4	5	6	7
Intimacy	1	2	3	4	5	6	7
Personal space	1	2	3	4	5	6	7
Respect	1	2	3	4	5	6	7
Rootedness	1	2	3	4	5	6	7
Security	1	2	3	4	5	6	7
Sex	1	2	3	4	5	6	7
Shared Activities	1	2	3	4	5	6	7
_____	1	2	3	4	5	6	7
_____	1	2	3	4	5	6	7

Now that you have completed your list, rank them in order of importance. Next, share the results with your wife. What needs do both of you identify as important? Discuss what needs are most important to you personally. As you discuss them, explain what that need means to you. Men and women often mean different things even when they use the same word (e.g., intimacy). Finally, discuss how each of your needs might change as you grow in marriage.

EXERCISE NINETEEN:
Identifying Your Hot Topics

This exercise will help you put your finger on those issues that are especially prone to cause conflict in your relationship. It will take about twenty minutes.

Listed below are the common relationship issues that most couples will encounter from time to time over the course of the relationship. Rate how much of a problem each issue is for you right now. If you wish to add other areas not included in our list, please do so. As always, do this on your own before discussing it with your wife.

	Not at all a problem						Very much a problem
Careers	1	2	3	4	5	6	7
Children	1	2	3	4	5	6	7
Chores	1	2	3	4	5	6	7
Communication	1	2	3	4	5	6	7
Friends	1	2	3	4	5	6	7
Illness	1	2	3	4	5	6	7
In-laws	1	2	3	4	5	6	7
Jealousy	1	2	3	4	5	6	7
Money	1	2	3	4	5	6	7
Priorities	1	2	3	4	5	6	7
Recreation	1	2	3	4	5	6	7
Relatives	1	2	3	4	5	6	7
Religion	1	2	3	4	5	6	7
Sex	1	2	3	4	5	6	7

Sleep habits	1	2	3	4	5	6	7
Her Ex-husband	1	2	3	4	5	6	7
My Ex-wife	1	2	3	4	5	6	7
_____	1	2	3	4	5	6	7
_____	1	2	3	4	5	6	7

Now that you have completed your list, share the results with your wife. What issues are "hot" for both of you, and what issues are "hot" for one or the other of you? Next, discuss what issues might become more troublesome in the future and what you can do to calm the conflict before it erupts.

Exercise Twenty:
Mind Reading

This exercise will help you bring true and false assumptions you are making about your wife into the open so there are fewer surprises and conflicts. It will take about ten minutes.

The next time you sense that your wife is upset with you, pause for a moment and say, "I want to read your mind." Then tell her what you think she was saying to herself. For example, "I think you are mad about the way I left the bed this morning," or "I think you are upset because I wanted to watch TV instead of take a walk." Then say, "How accurate am I?" Your wife can then rate how accurate you are on a percentage scale. For example, she might say, "That's about twenty percent accurate," or "That's one hundred percent accurate."

This simple exercise can be done anytime you sense that your wife is upset and you'd like to know if you are right about the reasons for it. Every couple mind reads every day. This exercise just makes that habit upfront and more useful.

EXERCISE TWENTY-ONE:
Sharing Withholds

This exercise will help you and your wife keep a clean emotional slate and avoid needless conflicts. We call it "sharing withholds" because it gives couples the chance to share thoughts and feelings that they have withheld from each other. It will take about ten to fifteen minutes.

Begin by writing two things your wife has done in the last forty-eight hours that you sincerely appreciated but did not tell her. For example, "I appreciate the compliment you gave me as I got out of the car yesterday" or "I appreciate the help you gave me in writing my proposal last night."

I appreciate … _____

I appreciate … _____

Next, write one thing your wife has done in the last forty-eight hours that irritated you but you did not say anything about. For example, "I didn't like it when you borrowed my umbrella without telling me" or "I didn't like it when you said nothing about the meal I prepared for us last night."

I didn't like it when … _____

Once both of you have written your statements, take turns sharing them. One person shares all three statements one after the other. Then the other person shares his or her three statements. And here is an important part of this exercise. The person on the receiving end can say only "thank you" after each statement. That's all. Just "thank you." This rule allows couples to share something that bugs them without fearing a blow-up or a defensive reaction. It also allows couples to receive critiques in the context of affirmation.

This exercise can be done every day. Once you get the hang of it, you don't need to write your statements down. All it takes is for one of you to say, "Do you want to share withholds?" Then each of you can take a moment to gather your thoughts, and away you go. Sharing withholds can save you hundreds of hours of needless bickering.

Exercise Twenty-Two:
Creating a Clean Slate

To paraphrase Ivy Baker Priest, the end may also be the beginning—if you start again with a clean slate. So if you are entering marriage for the second time, we want to help you do that through this workbook exercise.

Write a short history of your former relationship by completing the following sentence stems:

1. The things that initially attracted me to my first wife were . . .

   _____

2. I decided to marry my first wife because . . .

   _____

3. My first wife contributed to making our marriage work by . . .

   _____

4. I personally contributed to the relationship's difficulties by . . .

   _____

5. I still feel angry about . . .

   _____

6. I still feel guilty about . . .

   _____

7. I still feel sad about . . .

   _____

8. A lesson I've learned about marriage that I'll apply in my second marriage is . . .

   _____

9. What my first marriage taught me about myself is . . .

_____

Once you have taken the time to seriously contemplate and respond to each of these items, set aside some meaningful time to discuss them with your partner. If she has been married before, you can take turns responding to each of these items.

EXERCISE TWENTY-THREE:
Remarried with Children

So you are about to plunge into a new marriage that comes prepackaged with children. Are you ready? Most people would say you're not fully equipped until you've devised a plan. In this exercise we offer a way to get you started in doing just that.

Below is a list of important pointers for building a successful combined family. Read through the list and rank the top half-dozen items you feel are most important for you. It is important to do this on your own at first without influence from your partner.

- Start out in our own new place. This will eliminate turf squabbles, alleviate hurt feelings, and allow us to rid ourselves of the ghosts of the past.
- Ease into the relationships with our children and let them develop gradually. Relationships do not develop on demand. Trust takes time.
- Develop our own new traditions as a family. These will hasten our sense of belonging and connectedness as we develop familiar routines and special celebrations.
- Negotiate differences instead of fighting over right and wrong. Whether we let the dog sleep at the foot of the bed or in the garage is not a matter of right or wrong but simply a difference in preference.
- Maintain a special, planned, one-on-one time that allows our relationship to grow and be nourished in the midst of learning to parent together.
- Support our children's access to both biological parents. We do not want our children to be caught in the middle, nor do we want them to be emotionally torn apart.
- Adults in both households will make direct contact with each other to work out residential schedules with input from the children. We will not talk to each other through the children.

- We understand that much of a child's anger comes from changes and losses they have not chosen. Sharing a parent, a room, or toy with stepsiblings; going to a new school; missing your other parent, friends, and former neighborhood; having unfamiliar food; adjusting to new rules—all make for some guaranteed difficulties that we will work to understand.
- We will do all we can to learn about the dynamics of stepfamily situations. We will read books, talk to other stepparents, and attend seminars that will sharpen our skills as we work together as a parental team.
- Biological parents and ex-spouses will strive to be cooperative coparents with one another. We will compartmentalize our anger and hurt so we can cooperate on issues regarding the children's well-being. We know that if our conflict continues, the children will suffer.

Once you have ranked your items, compare notes with your partner. Discuss the items each of you checked and explain why. Then use these items to devise a plan for building your combined family together.

Exercise Twenty-Four:
Your Spiritual Journey

This exercise will help you and your wife share your individual pilgrimages. It will take about fifteen to twenty-five minutes.

Part of cultivating spiritual intimacy comes from merging two individual journeys. We are all beginners when it comes to spiritual development, but each of us has come from different places and traveled different roads to meet where we are today. You may have grown up in a religious home learning Bible verses, going to Sunday school, and studying at a Christian college. Or maybe you never went to church while growing up and are just becoming grounded in your faith. Whatever your story, take a moment to gather your thoughts about your own spiritual quest. Then make a few notes of some of the significant mile markers.

_____

_____

_____

_____

_____

_____

_____

Next, take a moment to complete this brief quiz.

Agree	Disagree	Spouses should ...
❒	❒	pray together every day
❒	❒	study the Bible together regularly
❒	❒	discuss spiritual issues

❐	❐	go to the same church
❐	❐	agree on theology
❐	❐	pay tithe
❐	❐	pray for each other
❐	❐	leave each other's spiritual life up to God
❐	❐	have the same level of spiritual maturity
❐	❐	attend church at least once a week

Once you have gathered your thoughts and completed the quiz, share your journey with your wife. Discuss what has brought you to where you are today. Also, compare how each of you responded to the quiz. Use it as a springboard to a deeper discussion of how each of you views spiritual matters.

Improving Your Serve

This exercise will help you and your wife cultivate a soulful marriage by reaching out to others. It will take about ten to fifteen minutes.

Here are a few of the ways couples have practiced the fine art of serving others:

- volunteering in a youth group
- supporting someone's education
- taking care of a shut-in's lawn
- welcoming new people to the neighborhood
- doing short-term relief trips overseas
- sending helpful books to people

Take a moment and list a few ways that you and your wife might reach out together as a team. Work on your own and be as creative as you can:

_____

_____

_____

_____

_____

_____

_____

_____

_____

Now compare your list with your wife's. Combine your lists and begin to rank the items in order of what both of you might like to do as a team. Once you have a couple things that seem like they might fit your joint style, discuss in more detail what they might actually look like. How would the two of you actually live out these forms of service? What do you think reaching out to others might do for your marriage?

EXERCISE TWENTY-SIX:
Study Your Spouse

This exercise will help you understand your wife's unique needs now and in the future. It will take about five to ten minutes *each day*.

No one can play as significant a role in encouraging your wife as you. No one can meet her needs better than you. But to be effective, you must study your wife by paying careful attention to her needs, desires, and aspirations.

This exercise is simply a prayer. It need not involve any sharing or discussion with your wife. It simply asks you to study and pray:

> God, our Creator, you were there when my wife was formed. You knit her together in her mother's womb. You know her every thought, need, and desire. You are acquainted with all her ways. Enlighten me. Teach me to know this complicated woman you have given me to love.

Record your observations below. How does your new understanding of your wife change the way you treat her?

_____

_____

_____

_____

_____

_____

_____

_____

_____

_____

_____

_____

_____

_____

_____

_____

_____

_____

_____

_____

_____

_____

_____

_____

_____

_____

Study your wife. Listen to her, talk to her. And every day, pray this simple prayer, asking God to help you understand her better.

Also from Les and Leslie Parrott

Becoming Soul Mates
Hardcover 0-310-20014-8
Softcover 0-310-21926-4

Meditations on Proverbs for Couples
Previously published as *Like a Kiss on the Lips*.
Hardcover 0-310-23446-8

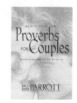

Love Is ...
Hardcover 0-310-21666-4

Marriage Devotional Bible
Hardcover	0-310-90133-2
Softcover	0-310-90878-7
Burgundy	
Bonded Leather	0-310-91120-6

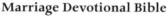

When Bad Things Happen to Good Marriages
Hardcover 0-310-22459-4
Workbook for Husbands 0-310-23902-8
Workbook for Wives 0-310-23903-6
Audio Pages™ 0-310-22977-4

Relationships
Hardcover 0-310-20755-X
Workbook 0-310-224381
Audio Pages™ 0-310-22435-7

Saving Your Marriage Before It Starts
Hardcover 0-310-49240-8
Workbook for Men 0-310-48741-2
Workbook for Women 0-310-48741-2
Audio Pages™ 0-310-49248-3
Curriculum Kit 0-310-20451-8
Leader's Guide 0-310-20448-8